DARK RIDE

Len Jenkin

BROADWAY PLAY PUBLISHING INC
New York
www.broadwayplaypublishing.com
info@broadwayplaypublishing.com

DARK RIDE

Cover art: *Autoskooter/Bunp Your Ass Off,* Len Jenkin
First printing, this edition: June 2015
I S B N: 978-0-88145-617-2

Book design: Marie Donovan
Page make-up: Adobe InDesign
Typeface: Palatino
Printed and bound in the U S A

DARK RIDE was first presented by the Soho Repertory Theatre, in New York City, on 12 November 1981. The cast was as follows:

TRANSLATOR .... David Brisbin
MARGO .... Melissa Hurst
JEWELLER .... Bill Sadler
THIEF .... Will Patton
WAITRESS .... Betty LaRoe
GENERAL .... Eric Loeb
ED .... Walter Hadler
EDNA .... Saun Ellis
MRS LAMMLE .... Joanne Akalaitis
MR ZENDAVESTA .... John Nesci

Director .... Len Jenkin
Set design .... John Arnone
Visual projections design .... Gerald Marks
Lighting design .... Bruce Porter
Costumes .... David C Woolard
Sound design .... Kathleen King
Stage manager .... Joanne McEntire

ACT ONE

1.

(Ride in: light, sound)

VOICE: Listen lady. If he's old enough to enjoy the ride, he's old enough to need a ticket...

2.

TRANSLATOR: My translation of *The Book of the Yellow Ancestor* is progressing very poorly. Ever since I began the work for this publisher of occult esoterica, I've suspected that something was seriously wrong. Possibilities: the text submitted to me was claimed to be a xerox copy of a parchment recently discovered in a cave in Szechwan Province, near Foo-Chow. How this document came into the possession of Mister Zendavesta of Sublime Publications he did not say. His response, when queried, is a genial grin. It is possible, then, that this text is fraudulent, or, if genuine, extremely corrupt. Either one of these theories is true, or—I'm somehow no longer able to make modern English sense out of ancient Chinese. In all honesty, with this text, it sometimes seems that I can no longer even read the language—brushstrokes seem like chicken scratchings in the sand.

Yet *The Book of the Yellow Ancestor* is definitely not composed of the kind of subtle or paradoxical discourse that could trouble the translator. Still, my tentative drafts all feel wrong—not nonsense, but off somewhere, at some angle....

I better explain. Actually, this Book of the Yellow Ancestor is not a book. It consists of one hundred and one fragments, which I assumed at first to be pithy phrases about life, or a set of directions for spiritual practices. Now I am not sure but that it is actually the journal of a housewife, equivalent to a laundry list, or the pointless travel diary of a garrulous lunatic, or a series of instructions for operating some partially biological machine that no longer exists.

The work of translation, as you might imagine, is confusingly dependent on my changing notions of these contexts.

Well, whatever the cause, there seem to be major blocks in the way of progress.

That's an understatement. The truth is that certain sections of the manuscript make me almost sure that either its a modern forgery, or that I'm going crazy. There's even one fragment...let me find it here... Ah—I've worked this passage over a dozen times, and it persists in coming out the same way. It seems to be describing a young woman reading some sort of popular novel. I quote. "Margo lies back on the couch in her apartment, and opens a book. She turns the pages slowly, until she finds her place. Her lips move slightly with the words she reads, like a child...."

3.

MARGO: Chapter Nine. At the Clinic. The man in bandages stands up slowly and walks over to the window. The sunlight is bright, and perhaps a ghost of it filters in through the layers of gauze that cover his face. But there's no need to speculate. Actually the light is felt by the man in bandages as heat ...nonspecific. He translates it into whatever suits him: this morning, a certain theatre in flames. Once his facial parts are sufficiently warm, he speaks to his visitor, a figure in white.

JEWELLER: I'm Ravensburg. I remember you, your voice, the smell of your hair—from long ago—or from a dream. I've dreamed every night since they brought me here. Who are you?

MARGO: The figure does not answer.

JEWELLER: He has robbed and beaten me. These bandages come off tomorrow, and then...WHO ARE YOU?

MARGO: Ravensburg says suddenly, with an unusual amount of emotion. The man in the next bed groans.

MAN: Unnnhh!

MARGO: Ravensburg continues.

JEWELLER: Here at the clinic they've treated me well. After the operation, they offered to spice my recuperation with all sorts of improvements. They offered plastic surgery, a new face—but I wanted to keep the scars. But you? What about you?

DOCTOR: Ah, there you are, number ten. You know you're not allowed out of the ward. Nurse—is anyone else disturbing the others?

MARGO: Enough book. Record player.

(Music)

MARGO: Stories about mental illness make me nervous. I keep thinking I'm a nurse at this clinic. It's actually a small sanitarium in the mountains. I'm a minor character who has her own little life...a boyfriend, a bicycle, a little house in the village…and I receive the major dramatic events, not in a direct and concerned way, but from a distance, like I'm overhearing two people I'll never see again, while I'm doing something else. Crazy, hah?

I've been jumpy since my boyfriend disappeared. Three weeks ago, he went out to sell something he found on the street—he finds things all the time—but he never came back. I thought he was dead or something, and I called every precinct, and then I called the hospitals.

Nobody ever heard of him. So I'm like a war bride or something, and then I get this postcard with a picture of some guy I don't even know on it. Can you believe it? "Dear Margo, I can't say where I am cause there's some people probably looking for me."

THIEF: I ran into some good luck and some trouble. I'll send for you.

MARGO: Send for me. He didn't even sign it, and I'm supposed to give up my job and go someplace? I can hardly stand living with him here where I got people I know. So now he's gonna write me from Cloud Cuckoo Land and say come on out the weather's fine. Pack your ermines, Margo. I love him but it's stupid, you know, like we have no idea how to love each other but we love each other anyway so we try but it comes out stupid.

Well, I've been nervous. I've been feeling that wherever I am, a certain someone else has been there just before me. Crazy, hah?

This card is postmarked Indianapolis, Indiana. You know what I think of when I think of Indianapolis, Indiana? It's like it reminds me of something that's not it…some other place that I don't particularly want to dream about…outskirts of some city, for miles alongside highways, feeding out into suburban streets....

4.

THIEF: Outskirts of some city, for miles alongside highways, feeding out into suburban streets, and I'm walking, and I keep looking back over my shoulder to see if anyone's behind me. I have the damn thing in a leather bag around my neck, and I'm heading south, and I figured I better...after three days on the road, I figured I better get inside somewhere, I figured I better eat something. I'm in America, coming into town. There's these long stretches of seedy apartment houses. Some people on the steps of one of them with a baby, and they're drinking beer, and they say hello out of the dark, and they don't even know who they're talking to, you know, but I say hello back anyway, and that seems to be it cause I just keep walking and they don't say anything else. O K. Now I'm really hungry but its a long way between neon, and then I see one coming, a red blur in the distance, and I squint at it, wanting it to say *Cafe* or *Eat Here* or something, but it ends up saying Tri-City Furniture or Red Robin Autos—Used But Not Abused—and finally I see another one, and it's a revolve, turning and turning, and it says THE EMBERS. We Never Close. So I go in. I'm here. Jukebox.

WAITRESS: Please wait to be seated.

THIEF: I'm seated. I'm in a chair at this table with this sugar and salt and pepper and a napkin and silverware—and I make sure the bag is hidden under my shirt. I got a menu, and I'm reading the section entitled: Burgers. Embers Burger-bacon cheese and tomato with our special sauce. Burger Hawaiian with zesty pineapple.

Burger Royale……

WAITRESS: You know what you want?

THIEF: Uh … yeah. A burger royale.

WAITRESS: Anything to drink?

THIEF: Yeah.

WAITRESS: What?

THIEF: Coffee.

WAITRESS: *(To kitchen)* Burger Royal.

ED: *(Cook)* Burger Royale.

THIEF: I'm still reading the menu to see if I made a mistake— Baked Meatloaf Viennese, mashed potatoes, mushroom sauce. Vegetables du jour: carrots and peas, cauliflower, creamed corn, and this guy comes out of the kitchen wearing this white apron, and he slides into the seat across from me.

ED: Hello, Slick.

THIEF: He says.

ED: Got a cigarette?

THIEF: I give him one and he says

ED: Thanks. You new here?

THIEF: Then I just look at him, and he looks back at me, and then he goes away.

I can see the T V, over the bar alongside the dining room. The waitress flips it on. It's in funny color like the tint knob's twisted, and she's tuned in to Outer Limits. O K. I like that. Then she changes the channel. Desert wind, billows of sand, straggly barbed wire. Zoom in past a dead camel covered with flies…on to a tattered tent. Inside, at a table covered with maps, sits this man in some kinda uniform, and he looks right at me

5.

GENERAL: Serving as field commander for a senile and capricious ruler is a thankless task. You are blamed for everything, though you simply follow orders. If you fail to develop the psychic strength necessary to deal with the intense and often obscure demands of the situation, you end up in the bird barracks, training seagulls to shit on the periscopes of enemy submarines. But you didn't come here to listen to me complain about my station in the service. No. You came to learn. I need not remind you that you'll require every bit of your knowledge out here. Simply to survive. Our position is hopeless. The enemy is everywhere. He has the material, the momentum, the cooperation of the natives, and time is on his side. We have only our brain power. Pay attention. Your life depends on it.
The reliability of incoming intelligence depends on two factors: the probable truth of the information itself, and the credibility of its source. Information that contradicts known facts has a low "probability of truth" rating. Think of an example.
Information coming from a notoriously unreliable source has a very low "probability of truth" rating. Think of an example.
Or from a source that could not conceivably have come into possession of the information. Think of an example.
Now. Even with a mass of scrupulously assessed information—where there is an enemy whose moves you must anticipate, decision making is complex. The Basic Rule: the more likely the enemy's action seems the less likely it becomes—as he will foresee that you will foresee it. He's clever. He'll change his plans—try to fool you. Therefore, the less likely the enemy's action seems, the more likely it is that he'll resort to exactly

that strategem. If it seems impossible—it's certain. Think of an example.
We are moving out at dawn to attack point B. I am presently sending out false information that we intend to attack point A. I am also giving out information that we will attempt to convince the enemy that we are going to attack point B. If the enemy should intercept any of our real communiques in regard to our target B, rather than the false ones concerning A, they will think that those actually genuine pieces of information are only part of the attempt to deceive them.
I receive many intelligence reports on the enemy daily. I cross file them carefully in my Book of Intelligence. I attempt to assess their relevance and truth. However, I have not seen the enemy themselves for quite some time—years. But I understand their strategy in this. They wish to convince me that this is all some kind of game. Once this speculation has hold of my mind, and I relax my vigilance, they'll be on me like sewer rats, ripping at my throat. But, of course…

6.

TRANSLATOR: You see. You torture your mind to find modern equivalents for what seems to be ancient wisdom, and you end up revealing the seemingly obscure conversations of military officers, or peasants, hotel-keepers, fishermen, senile nuns at roadside shrines. Its indicative of the fate of serious scholarship in our time that, for the pittance Mister Zendavesta pays me, I continue to struggle with this impossibly recalcitrant text.
However, there is one dim light. Structure. I'm fairly sure this book presupposes, as a frame device, the existence of a group of companions, who were originally ten in number. Whether these characters

relate to actual people, or are pure inventions, I have no idea. The author seems obsessed with their moving from place to place like peripatetic shadows.
The Chinese setting itself is also subject to debate: I've come to believe it may well be a fiction. I'm almost certain that the book relies on geographical information about China plagiarized from a certain *Child's Picture Atlas of the World*...though at times the author seems to have either misread this source, or is deliberately inventing locations which never existed.
Yet this Book of the Yellow Ancestor remains somehow fascinating. I understate the case. I have been up all night with it for days. I think of nothing else. It has even crossed my mind that this text may be identical to one or more of the fabled "hidden" books: The Book of the Black Pilgrimage—or the Book of Brightness of Rabbi Isaac the Blind, or even—the legendary Epistle of Illusion and Caution.
It's even crossed my mind that Chinese may not be its original language...that this work in front of me is itself a translation, or a translation of a translation...of a translation

7.

WAITRESS: Will that be all?

THIEF: What?

WAITRESS: You having dessert?

THIEF: Uh, yeah. Gimme some pie.

WAITRESS: Apple, cherry, lemon meringue? Key lime, rhubarb, pecan, peach, pumpkin? Boston cream?

ED: I quit.

WAITRESS: You're breaking my heart. Where you going?

ED: I'm southbound. *(He is dragging what looks like the body of a man wrapped in brown paper and string. Ticket windows.)*

TICKET SELLER: What's the situation?

ED: Through the sharp hawthorn blows the cold wind.

TICKET SELLER: Too bad. What are you doing about it?

ED: Going south.

TICKET SELLER: How many?

ED: Party of one.

TICKET SELLER: If that thing's gonna ride, it needs a ticket.

ED: It'll fit on my lap.

TICKET SELLER: The hell it will. Pay or walk.

*(*ED *checks his money. Not enough)*

ED: They used to let John ride the hound for free. Travelled everywhere with him. But this is sweet goodbye. You people are in luck. Deep Sea Ed is caught short here, so I gotta unload my prize possession: the genuine preserved and mummified body of John Wilkes Booth, the most famous assassin of all time. I got the papers and everything. Affidavits from doctors. Got 'em framed—some of 'em. I got an x-ray photo of the fractured leg where he hit the stage floor. Even got a ring. You can mention that he swallowed it while attempting to disguise himself as he ran. You found it in the mummy's stomach. Even got a B on it. Get it? B for Booth.

Look, you can make it over Egyptian if you want. Rig it with a battery so it wiggles. Jesus. You people don't know what you're looking at. This attraction took in five hundred dollars a day last season. You do that good with what you're showing? John Wilkes here makes money when everything else on the lot is

dead. I built the fucker, and I'da run him all winter in a goddamn storefront if I didn't have to go back to Canada. My mother's in a fucking clinic in fucking Winnipeg, and you people are hassling me.
Look, I don't know what kind of trade you got, but if it ain't fun and fulfilling, try the show business. Hey, I'm begging you. Take him off my hands. All right. I made my offer, you turned me down. I ain't saying you won't regret it, cause you will. *(To* TICKET SELLER*)* Gimme one.

TICKET SELLER: Winnipeg?

ED: Hell, no. Look, can I leave something in the baggage claim? I'll be back to pick it up in a few days...

WAITRESS: Will that be all?

THIEF: What else you got?

WAITRESS: Jello.

(Jello music)

THIEF: I'll have some of that jello.

WAITRESS: Red? Or green? Red? Or green?

THIEF: I was telling you, I'm running away, cause I went over my head, you know. I mean I grabbed something good, real good—and I don't know what to do with it. It's the kind of thing—you had it and somebody took it—you'd kill people to get it back. See, I had a ring I found somewhere, so I'm looking to sell it, and I hear about a guy in an office building...I'm in this corridor, see...wandering around, somebody's playing a radio behind one of these doors....

8.

JEWELLER: I am a dealer in precious stones. This particular favorite of mine first turned up in India in 1712. Supposedly, the raw stone was ripped from the forehead of an Indian idol, and came into the hands of a trader from Sumatra, who was promptly torn to pieces by a pack of rabid dogs. But that, of course, is hearsay.

Louis the Fourteenth is said to have given it to the lovely Madame Montespan as a mark of royal favor, which she lost soon afterwards. She became a nun at a Spanish convent, where she is rumored to have been badly mistreated by the sisters… It appeared again in London in 1847 as the stickpin of Prince Ivan Kanitovsky, who was murdered by a bellboy at the Connaught Hotel. Abdul Hamid of Turkey possessed it briefly until he was dethroned, and it was sold to Simon Montharides, whose carriage was dragged over a cliff by shying horses near the Borgo Pass, killing him, his wife, and two children. What a coincidence. The stone was then placed by his executors in the Green Vaults of Dresden, which will be mentioned more than once this evening. The American actress who purchased it in 1930 was burned to death in the tragic fire at the Bijou theatre in Los Angeles. I bought it from her attorneys in 1971.

When I came into possession, the stone had its original Indian design. An idiotic waste. This first cutting and faceting had been done in Venice by Joseph Asscher. The months of tension preceding his botch of the job caused him to be hospitalized for a nervous disability…a small sanitarium near the Grand Canal. Still there, I believe…

The decision of how to cleave and cut the stone so as to reveal its full power was the most difficult of my life. My final decision was the right one. The stone is now

a triple cut brilliant, with one hundred and one facets around its table. I did this.
I have possessed this stone for ten years now. I spend each night alone with it.

THIEF: So I'm in this corridor, see, wandering around this office building. I know the guy's name, but I don't remember the office number. I try one.

JEWELLER: Yes?

THIEF: Mister Ravensburg?

JEWELLER: Yes, I am Ravensburg.

THIEF: I'm here to sell something. A ring. It's a family heirloom.

JEWELLER: I buy nothing.

THIEF: But I was told you could help me out.

JEWELLER: I do not buy anything.

THIEF: You don't buy anything tonight?

JEWELLER: Not tonight, not ever.

THIEF: It's my mother's wedding ring. This guy Bernard, he sent me. You know Bernard?

JEWELLER: I do not have the honor.

THIEF: Then I guess there's a mistake here. I'm looking for a Mister Ravensburg.

JEWELLER: I am Mister Ravensburg.

THIEF: But you don't buy anything.

JEWELLER: No. Here we do cutting and shaping.

THIEF: Hey, maybe there's someone else in this building named Ravensburg.

JEWELLER: No doubt. In this building, it's a very common name.

*(*JEWELLER *turns away, the* THIEF *grabs him from behind, knocks him down. A scream. The* THIEF *steals the diamond. Blackout. Music of distant Motel)*

9.

EDNA: You know how to read? Words? No vacancy.

THIEF: I can read—but there's nothing else for miles. I thought I'd ask you personally….

*(*EDNA *looks him over.)*

EDNA: I happen to have one room I always leave empty. Room ten. The last guy I put in there—pool hustler from Grand Forks, North Dakota—died in his sleep. He died of a dream.

THIEF: Well, that's too bad, but I'll lie down anywhere. Besides, I didn't know him. His ghost won't trouble me.

EDNA: Good enough. *(Hands key)* You woke me up, so tell me some lies. What are you doing here?

THIEF: Well there's a man in town that won't be happy till he sells me a dog. I gotta see him.

EDNA: Good.

THIEF: Thanks. Uh, I don't like to bother you, but you got something to ear? A sandwich and a beer or something…I can pay you

EDNA: Sorry. Usta have a coffee shop. "24 hours. We never close." My husband ran it. Cook, and a good one too. But every time he gets twenty bucks in his pocket he thinks it's time to see the world. Bastard's been gone for six months this time. He'll come back—but I don't suggest you wait up for him. Everything's in the room—towels, magazines. And if you get lonely, don't ring my bell. *(She is gone.)*

THIEF: But I want you people to understand that running scared isn't my full-time occupation. I mean, your mind keeps working too. I'm a writer. I write Margo postcards. And I read—magazines. You can read a lot of interesting things in magazines. This one here is the *U F O Review,* published by Sublime Publications, and its got articles like "I was transported to Venus," and "Platillo Volador! Saucer over Brazil."

(By the end of this speech the THIEF *is seated, and* EDNA *appears to sit alongside him—two lawn chairs.)*

EDNA: Fascinating. Listen, I know you're running. Why don't you run with me. I got a little sideline I take out on the road. Deep Sea Edna's Shooting Gallery and Marine Museum. You'll do for setup and takedown. You can feed the fish.

THIEF: Well, I might be better off on my own. I could bring trouble.

EDNA: Trouble's a friend of mine. Stay in your tracks, whoever's looking for you'll find you sure. Probably stab you in your sleep behind a billboard. Go down my road for a while, you'll disappear. Besides, you can help me look around.

THIEF: For what?

EDNA: For Ed.

THIEF: But I don't know anything about fish.

EDNA: Don't worry. I have an eye for talent. And if people are looking for you, get a disguise ... pair of glasses or something. We leave in the morning. Southbound. *(She exits.)*

THIEF: But in case you people think I'm only interested in the sensational—there's another article in this magazine that's different. I been thinking about it—reading it over and over. It's by a Mrs Carl Lammle, who is someone I'd like to talk to sometime. Its called:

ALL: THE WORLD OF COINCIDENCE.

10.

MRS LAMMLE: All of you are, I'm sure, familiar with what I term the WORLD OF COINCIDENCE. In this world, events seem to be more connected…than they are in our everyday world, where they most often seem random, absurd—if not perniciously unrelated to each other. In the world of coincidence, however, the most common expression is:

ALL. What a coincidence!

MRS LAMMLE: For example:

MAN: Excuse me, sweetheart, you dropped your fish…I mean…scarf.

WOMAN: Thanks, mister… *(To herself)* …Odd he should say that. Last night I dreamed of a fish.

MRS LAMMLE: Or…

MAN: Excuse me, sweetheart, you dropped your scarf…I mean…fish.

WOMAN: Thanks, mister. Odd he should say that. Last night I dreamed of a scarf.

MRS LAMMLE: Of course.

OTHER MAN #1: I was in the middle of writing my chapter on wind-force, when a sudden breeze blew my papers all over the room.

OTHER MAN #2: Remarkable. *(To himself)* Odd that he should say that. Last night I dreamed of papers, blowing all around me….

MRS LAMMLE: Yes. Our common idea of cause and effect is succinctly illustrated in the common expression: "Just one thing after another." This notion is linked to our childish ideas of the nature of space and time. In the World of Coincidence, these ideas are null, and void. In man's original mind, as we find it among primitive peoples, space and time have a very precarious existence. They become fixed concepts only in the course of our mental development. Actually, the truth is, that in themselves, space and time consist of nothing. They are only concepts born of the discriminating activity of the conscious mind. They do, however, form the indispensable coordinates for describing bodies in motion. Think of an example. A ball rolling down an incline, a man travelling south along a certain highway...

Lets get on with it, shall we. I have been keeping a personal journal of coincidence for thirty years. After a very fruitful year or two, the question arises forcefully in the seeking mind...was I simply more aware of coincidences by keeping this journal—or was I making them happen?

In any case, some convincing examples from the collection: You ask me, what were the names of the three men who murdered Doctor Berry at Green Hill? Ed Green, Fred Berry and Ted Hill. FACT. John McCabe of Fulham Road in the Bronx, New York was listening to a record of Cry of the Wild Goose by Frankie Laine....

(Music: I must go where the wild goose goes, I must fly where the wild goose flies...)

MRS LAMMLE: ...when a Canadian goose crashed through his bedroom window. FACT.

As the Danforth family of Peru, Indiana were watching the sinking of the *Titanic* on a T V movie of the week, just as the iceberg hits the ship, a large block of ice falls through the roof of their ranch style home, smashes the T V to smithereens. FACT.

Alphonso Bedoya was crossing Prince's Canal in Amsterdam. He was struck and killed by a green taxi carrying a passenger named Ravensburg. His brother, Armando Bedoya, was also struck and killed, in Amsterdam, while crossing Prince's Canal, by a green taxi—carrying a passenger named Ravensburg—ten years later. FACT.

At times an expert witness has coincidentally been present at the scene of the coincidental, as when Doctor A D Bajkov, the noted ichthyologist, visiting the United States, was bombarded with fish from the sky, shortly after breakfast in Biloxi, Mississippi. FACT

But let's take a more ordinary example. Let's say you decide to go to the oculist to get a pair of glasses. You walk into the shop, past the displays of glasses and frames in the window. A bell rings. Once inside, you notice that the oculist's shop seems also to be an outlet for the books of a company called Sublime Publications

11.

TRANSLATOR: Introducing Mister Zendavesta, my employer in this suspect venture. He should have just finished his usual breakfast: quail eggs in which the blebs of fertilization are kept raw, lace cake, jompoo juice, and jello. As the fisherman can infer the presence of the great whale from a single bubble on the sea—so Mister Zendavesta claims to be able to discern the….

ZENDAVESTA: The Book of the Yellow Ancestor! The translation! You've finished!

TRANSLATOR: Are you joking?

ZENDAVESTA: The wisdom of the Yellow Ancestor is no joking matter. You're almost finished?

TRANSLATOR: I've made some headway. But this text still seems extremely unreliable.

ZENDAVESTA: Unreliable to you—perhaps a rock of sanity to me. Forge ahead. Translate! What have you got so far?

TRANSLATOR: Well, there are some completed sections, but they're really…odd.

ZENDAVESTA My ears are yours.

TRANSLATOR: O K…I'm fairly sure about this one—"The Genii's Pharmacy—prescription ten. Feed a small duckling on rose petals, mixed with oil and blood. When the bird is grown and its feathers come out red, kill it, dry it, crush it, feathers and all, and take a teaspoon of this powder every day for three hundred days."

ZENDAVESTA: That's it?

TRANSLATOR: That section, yeah.

ZENDAVESTA: And for what condition is this the cure?

TRANSLATOR: It doesn't say.

ZENDAVESTA: Of course.

TRANSLATOR: I might be mistaken about the characters for prescription. Perhaps "document" or "dispatch" …I also had trouble with…

ZENDAVESTA: Please. Sublime Publications owes you a debt it can never repay. Your photo on the jacket? A certainty. Tell me, are there any passages that seem to be directions to a place?

TRANSLATOR: Not yet.

ZENDAVESTA: Keep at it. Don't fail me. I'm leaving shortly for the Oculists Convention near Mexico City. I'm sure you'll be kind enough to meet me there. We'll work together by the pool. A change of scene might calm your fevered brain. Your ticket.

(THIEF *rings the bell.)*

THIEF: Anybody here?

ZENDAVESTA: *(To* TRANSLATOR.*)* Excuse me. A customer. Wait here. Browse. *(To* THIEF*)* Yes?

THIEF: I want to get a pair of clear glasses with just glass in them, you know.

ZENDAVESTA: I know. Read the top line please.

THIEF: I can't make any sense of that.

ZENDAVESTA: Fine. Lie down. This will only take a moment.

(As ZENDAVESTA *examines the* THIEF:*)*

TRANSLATOR: Zendavesta used to be an optical lens grinder in Chicago. He lived in a small room at the Diamond Hotel. He was a bachelor. He thought a lot about the nature of this life we lead, and his own particular destiny. He often lay awake nights, turning these two questions over in his mind like dice in a cage. One day he was walking down West Madison Street after work, when he saw a man wearing a sandwich board sign, which read: WE LIVE INSIDE. The man was selling a pamphlet for ten cents, also titled WE LIVE INSIDE. The lens-grinder bought a copy. Years later he could be heard to remark:

ZENDAVESTA: I read it in bed, and before I fell asleep that night, I was inside.

THIEF: What'd you say?

ZENDAVESTA: *(To* THIEF*)* Ah! Just as I suspected. The green quinsy. Invariably leads to blindness and insanity. This condition requires an immediate surgical procedure.

THIEF: Hey, look. I just…

ZENDAVESTA: Stop. I know what you think. I can anticipate your query. The answer is: would I tell you you needed an operation if you didn't?

THIEF: I'll take my chances. Gimme the glasses and I'll get out of here.

ZENDAVESTA: Perhaps you'd like to purchase a new face, something so attractive that social graces will become unnecessary? You'll be able to get away with it, if you follow me....

THIEF: No thanks. I'll be going now.

ZENDAVESTA: Just a moment. You seem like a malleable young man, who's in trouble. I'm preparing an expedition, and am currently attempting to hire a muscular assistant who's not bright enough to cause any harm.
I have sent every senator and representative in the Congress of our United States a registered letter, on the letterhead of Sublime Publications, appealing for immediate financing to .equip us for the adventure. As soon as these funds arrive, we depart.
I'll take you where jewellers and policemen will never find you. We'll even send for Margo.

THIEF: Margo? How do you know...

ZENDAVESTA: Where are we going, you ask? Young man, the new cosmogony has been revealed to me. The key is simple. We live inside the earth. Modern astronomers are perfectly correct, except that they have everything inside out. The entire cosmos is like an egg. We live on the inner surface of a hollow shell, and inside the hollow are the sun, the moon, the stars, the planets, and the comets in their courses. What, you ask, is outside the shell? Nothing. Absolutely nothing. The inside is all there is.
However, at a certain point in the shell, there is a hole. A tiny hole, through which a man could enter that endless effluvium of endless absence, to annihilate himself in bliss. I'm talking to you about the resurrection, with a difference.

THIEF: Yeah…

ZENDAVESTA: As soon as the exact location of this hole is revealed, the funds assembled, we set out. We have, of course, been subjected to insolent ridicule in our attempts to bring this knowledge before the, public..

THIEF: You ever think about U F Os?

ZENDAVESTA: The things you call unidentified flying objects are neither objects, nor flying, nor unidentified. We know very well who they are. *(Bell)*

ZENDAVESTA: Wait here. Browse.

THIEF: *(To* TRANSLATOR.*)* You read these books?

TRANSLATOR: Some of them.

THIEF: They interesting?

TRANSLATOR: Some of them.

THIEF: Tell him 1 couldn't stay, hah. And good luck with your expedition.

TRANSLATOR: I doubt I'll be going … Hey! What's your name?

(The THIEF *is gone.)*

ZENDAVESTA: *(To* MRS LAMMLE*)* Yes?

MRS LAMMLE: I'm not interested in your philosophy. I want to pick up a pair of glasses.

ZENDAVESTA: Name?

MRS LAMMLE: Mrs Carl Lammle.

TRANSLATOR: Mister Zendavesta claims to have the world's most complete library of the occult, excepting only the collection stored in the Green Vaults of Dresden. Maybe there's a manuscript copy of *The Book of Brightness*, or *The Epistle of Illusion and Caution*… Hmmm…"*Nine Holes of Jade*", by Soo Ling, "the candid memoirs of a Hong Kong call girl". … Here's one called *"Venus in India"*, by a Captain Ernest Devereaux, "the amorous adventures of a gallant soldier"...

This one's got an odd frontispiece. Looks like an engraving of a long corridor, anonymous office building. One door is partly open, and I can see a small room within. A man sits at a table, a safe behind him, diamond dust and oil coat his fingers.

12.

JEWELLER: I am the dealer in precious stones. I know them, their sounds, their crystal hums.

GENERAL: *(Writing)* Crystal hums

JEWELLER: I am a patient man. I studied in Amsterdam for ten years to learn to mark the stones for the chisel. Ten more years to cleave. Place the chisel, kiss it, and the stone falls into its parts. Like men. One tap, and into parts invisible. Now the stone I love has been stolen from me, and I will have it back, and I will wash it clean in the thief's blood.
I'll explain myself, if you don't mind. I met a girl once. She was a Dutch girl, and she worked in a bookstore in Amsterdam, on Prince's Canal. Children's books. She also played the flute in an amateur orchestra. I came to buy a book in English for my brother's son in America. For his birthday. She helped me choose. I chose one about a monkey.

GENERAL: ...a monkey...

JEWELLER: I stared at her the whole time. She was not embarrassed. We had coffee.
She loved me. When I tell it to you now it is difficult, even for me who lived it, to believe. For one year, she brought me into the world. We went to cafes, the theatre, even to the countryside. At home, she would

watch as I marked the stones. She was quiet, and asked for nothing. I thought I was reborn under a new sun. One night she met the conductor of the state symphony at a party at the university. One week later she went to live with him in a house in a suburb of Amsterdam. For a month, I could nor believe this simple truth. Her smell was everywhere.

After she moved away, I cut the stone. It had arrived a year ago, and I had spent months delaying, staring at it as she watched me. I always felt that my mark was wrong, and if I cut—the stone would fall into worthless fragments. That night, I opened the Zohar to the Book of Brightness, and though I read it without understanding, it calmed me. I erased my mark. And then I bled from my nose and mouth, and the blood flowed down onto the stone, a translucent coat of my blood, and the stone shone clearer than ever. I remember the open Zohar, the blood, the light, the diamond dust from the polisher, the view out over the canals, the passing boats of the tourists. Then, almost without my noticing—the tap of the hammer on the blade.

Once I spent my nights looking into the facets of the stone to see the past, the future, and the roads between. Now I can only look into my mind's picture of it. The blue glow fills my skull. I can't find the thief, but I see something he'll follow as I follow the stone. Do you see it, general? See it.

GENERAL: *(Aside.)* This private work can be distressing to a professional soldier. *(To* JEWELLER*)* Right, sir. Just give me the information. Well screw the enemy to the wall.

JEWELLER: Into the tenth facet! An apartment in this city! She's dreaming, and she thinks my eye is something in her dream. She wakes, opens a novel .... odd book, must read it sometime. She closes the book.

She turns on the TV. Perfect. General, get your hat and stick. We have work to do.

13.

MARGO: My Sony is a one-way communication system, sending me words and pictures that never end. They're always changing, and despite this, I always understand them. My T V can communicate with me, if I'm awake, and watching. To communicate with me means to say stuff, or show me stuff I understand. If you say something to me I don't understand, we're not communicating, are we? If I say something to you and you don't understand, we're not communicating. Are we? But we're communicating right now.
If we keep communicating like this—so we understand each other—it'll only lead to little ripples in our context, this world of common words and pictures that allows us to communicate in the first place. Like me and my T V—it never does much more than give a little shuffle to the cards I've already got. It's pleasant, but now I'm turning it off. I need a new deck.

JEWELLER: General, do something. I'm not interested in her philosophy.

GENERAL: Why don't you forget everything you know about all that and let us get on with it.

MARGO: If you step out of this pleasant sensation of understanding, and the world that makes it possible, you stop communicating. These postcards from my lover are perfect: notes from somewhere else torn up and delivered by the wind.

GENERAL: Why don't you forget everything you know about all that and let us get on with it...

MARGO: I miss the crazy bastard. I did book—I did T V —now record player.

(Music)

GENERAL & JEWELLER: Gotcha!

*(*MARGO *screams.)*

END OF ACT ONE

(Intermission)

ACT TWO

14.

(EDNA, MARCELLA, MARGO, *and* MRS LAMMLE)

MRS LAMMLE: Yes. Our Bible is a deep mine of treasure for the student of coincidence. The Book of Revelation lists ten plagues, ten seals, and ten archangels: Michael, Gabriel, Zakiel, Uriel, Jamalel, Nuriel, Samael, Raziel, Ariel and last, but not least, Fleuriel. And how many heads has Babylon, the mother of harlots? Ten. FACT. One particular jewel in this mine is the story of Jonah. The prophet's dark ride in the belly of the whale—three days. Christ's tenure in the tomb before his resurrection—three days. FACT.
And now, from my journal. Twenty years ago, when she was four years old, a young woman, who shall remain anonymous, stood quietly outside a gypsy fortune telling parlor in Chicago, while her mother had her palm read. The gypsy, a certain Madame Edna. ...Marcella, would you bring out the model, please? Thank you, Marcella. The gypsy, a certain Madame Edna, gave the girl a charlotte russe, insisting that she try it.

EDNA: Try it.

MRS LAMMLE: She loved it. Recently, the girl saw her second charlotte russe, in the window of an expensive restaurant. When she entered and ordered it, she found that the charlotte russe was reserved for a special customer—Madame Edna, looking exactly the same after all these years. They shared the charlotte russe, and both seemed astonished at meeting once again over the same confection.

At some time in the future, this young woman attends a formal banquet near Mexico City. To her surprise it features charlotte russes as dessert. Meanwhile, Madame Edna herself has been invited to another, rather less formal affair in the basement of the same hotel. She loses her way in the maze of the building's corridors, knocks on a door to ask for directions. Our young woman, holding a charlotte russe in her hand, opens it. They stare at each other. What a coincidence.

I still tell these stories, but I'm no longer sure what they signify. Perhaps I'm tired. I want to get away for a while—from Carl—that's my husband—and my life here. Lately, I've been dreaming of trains—little locomotives, with pleasant curls of smoke twirling into blue skies, crossing little child's maps of the continent, heading south to some resting place under a new sun. I need a vacation.

15.

GENERAL: Hmmm. A dispatch from the front. Thank you, Marcella. Perhaps a notice of promotion. Recognition of my efforts at our particularly exposed station is long overdue.

However, it's possible that the news enclosed will take a grimmer turn. Battle statistics. The valor of my second in command has long been suspect....

The truth is that I left the station in charge of my waterboy, whose command of English is far from...but why speculate? The applicable rule in these complex situations: never assume you know where you're

going, till you've gotten there. In other words, you've got to suck it and see. *(Opens envelope)*
Hmmmrn. It seems that in my absence our position has been overrun by the enemy, the remainder of our unit, destroyed, and my personal possessions burnt to ashes. I have been reassigned to the bird barracks. "Report immediately."
I refuse. As you've seen, I am already embarked on a new career. I am a kidnapper. However, this is not as tawdry as it sounds. Margo actually behaves as if we're taking her on holiday. In any case, as Mussolini said to the British ambassador when their limousine ran over a child in the streets of Naples... "Never look back."
This adventure will also serve as a snazzy final fillip to my memoirs. Memoirs with a difference. Not only my actual experience in the service, but my dreams, fantasies—the inner man. And I have developed a .compositional technique. Among all the methods of writing, I may not be certain my own way is the best, but I am absolutely sure it is the most religious. I begin by writing the first sentence, and trust to almighty God for the second.
But let's be frank for a moment. This jeweller is a madman. When he returned from this private clinic in the mountains, his imagination was diseased. However, he's paying me. His plan? Now that we've kidnapped the girl, we follow the postcards she receives from this thief to track him down. Then we use her as bait to draw him into our figurative maw.
We get train tickets
We head south.
We cross over the border into Mexico.
We race through the desert, its stark beauty interrupted by an occasional panorama of local business: Panchito's Tacos, Valdez auto-repair. The jeweller is abstracted. Margo is resigned...or pleased. She knows

we're taking her to him. She cannot imagine what this jeweller plans to do to her lover, once we find him.

CONDUCTOR: Tickets? Tickets?

JEWELLER: Why don't you ask the engineers in the locomotive for their tickets?

CONDUCTOR: Because they're driving the train.

JEWELLER: So are we.

MARGO: Right.

JEWELLER: She's a quick study.

GENERAL: I examine the final postcard for clues. Seems to be a souvenir card from some seedy roadside attraction. The thief must be gone from there. Postmark is ten days old...We rush on toward the posh hotel outside Mexico City, where the Jeweller has engaged a number of ballrooms to bait our trap.

MARGO: So this is Mexico.

JEWELLER: Yes.

MARGO: It's just what I thought it would be. I've seen it on T V... Dead cows.

JEWELLER: Do you love me?

MARGO: Love you? You're kidnapping me. Besides, I don't even know you. I mean maybe if I knew you for years or something, I doubt it. No.

JEWELLER: You may change your mind. You may discover that love is not so much a feeling...as it is a situation.

GENERAL: Though this thief seems both dangerous and resourceful, my jeweller is confident he'll rise to the bait, like a great whale coming up from the bottom of the sea.

JEWELLER: Confident? No. Certain. I had the stone, and it brought me the evil fate to lose it. Now I pursue, but he has the stone, and the weight of its power slows him, his legs grow heavy, his alertness dwindles, and we have him! Only a man of learning and restraint can possess the stone without it leading him to his doom.

GENERAL: Right. Hmmm. The picture on this latest postcard is curious. In it is a badly lettered sign, that clearly once said DEEP SEA ED'S WORLD OF WONDERS, but two new letters—N-A, have been squeezed in after ED…

16.

EDNA: You curious about love?

THIEF: Yeah.

EDNA: Psst. Here's the secret. It's a mystery. The truth is that loving Ed is just something I do, you know. I don't think about it anymore. He was the original owner of this popgun palace and marine museum. When I met him he specialized in window sleeps, went into trances in store windows to advertise furniture sales. "Suspended animation. Hasn't eaten for two weeks!" He was doing it at Watson Discount. After Mom was asleep, one, two in the morning—I'd go down there and slip food to him, bags fulla greasy tacos, sneaking down Main Street like a thief. I was seventeen… When he left town, I left with him. You still don't know what the hell to do, do you?

THIEF: Well, I'm still trying to hide….

EDNA: Get a straight job. That'll hide you. Nobody looks at working people. My brother's got a body shop in Las Cruces. That's on the border. Means the crosses.

THIEF: I don't know anything about the insides of cars. I don't really know how to do anything.

EDNA: Then go into show business. Take that girl along. She could do the parachuting, which is easy for women and they enjoy it too. Gives 'em a thrill. I used to do it with Ed. Last time was a state fair in Jackson, Mississippi. I lost myself up there, landed in an empty gondola heading east. I stopped jumping after that, and Ed was scared, so we got a Mexican kid named Eduardo. Lot of style. Made himself up a batman suit. He did one season with us. Next year some circus picked him up. Took him to Europe. His luck didn't hold. He was doing his batman jump in Venice when his shrouds tangled and that was it. Never had a chance. Batman into the Grand Canal.
For a while, me and Ed were big time. Owned a carnival on the Canadian circuit, even did the Winnipeg Provincial Fair. Had a Hall of History, all kinds of figures in dramatic tableaus.
Looked realer than hell. Ed made them all himself. Paper maché and spit.
And then Ed got religion. He invented a new ride for the midway, his idea being that its motion would provide a spiritual experience for the clientele. It was called the Ezekial, and that's what it looked like: wheel in a wheel, way in the middle of the air. The little wheel run by faith, and the big wheel run by the grace of God…. Well, on its first run with live customers some drunk teenager flies out of the damn thing. Ed is sued by these lawyers, and he loses everything—his carnival, the Ezekial ride, everything. Then he disappeared. When I found him again he was a fry cook at a place called the Embers.

ED: Here's your two over light, I got a burger royale working…

EDNA: It was back then that we started doing the casket of death. Ten sticks of dynamite, lead shielding, some cotton in your ears, a bag of stage blood, and they faint in the seats. When we were testing, I learned something. Best thing I can teach you. We'd light the fuse and walk away. It'd burn down in about five minutes, but sometimes it seemed like an hour waiting for the charge to go off. That's what kills people. Time seems stretched. They figure the fuse has gone out, they go back to-check, and are right on top of it when she blows. I learned to give it plenty of time…

MAN: I'm not interested in philosophy. We want to see the fish. One, please.

EDNA: Hey Mister. If she's old enough to enjoy the show, she's old enough to need a ticket. Take 'em in.

(The THIEF *is gone with the customers.)*

ZENDAVESTA: Are you showing people to these fish, or vice-versa.

EDNA: Cute. Think it over. You're the one who paid at the door.

ZENDAVESTA: Yes, indeed. Should I be amused, or is this somehow educational?

EDNA: Educational. These fish are quiet, and besides, they know the secrets of the deep.

ZENDAVESTA: Do you mind if I sit down a moment, the better to contemplate these marvels.

EDNA: Help yourself.

ZENDAVESTA: I am Mister Zendavesta, a humble explorer of the etheric borderlands. I'd appreciate it if you'd examine this small pamphlet, entitled WE LIVE INSIDE. You might find it instructive.

EDNA: Tell me if I have this right. You are a harmless crank.

ZENDAVESTA: Crank? Madam, I deplore cranks. The discoverer of the corpuscular theory of sounds, of kinematic relativity, of the cosmic donut, where are they now? Already dead, and buried alongside the Mad Hatter. I am a scientist.

EDNA: F\I'm proud of you. But I'm closing up now.

ZENDAVESTA: Please. I know what you think.

EDNA: Do you now?

ZENDAVESTA: Of course. There are two sides to every argument, and both of them are mine. You see, I was once a common voluptuary like yourself. Yet I soon realized that the ordinary mines of enjoyment are easily exhausted. I perceived that these twisted paths of pleasure turned back on themselves in diminishing spirals of decreasing delight. Once I had escaped the toils of the serpent of desire, my mind opened. Ideas descended on me like a flight of vultures on a dying antelope.
You're quite a handsome woman, you know. I've been looking for a group of brave companions to set out on a certain expedition I have in mind....

EDNA: Sorry. I gotta babysit that night.

ZENDAVESTA: Then perhaps something less total in its implications. I am also the entertainment coordinator at the upcoming World Oculists' Convention at the extraordinary Hacienda Ramon on the outskirts of Mexico City. Perhaps you'd consent, for a fee, of course, to display these fish in some suitable....

17.

JEWELLER: Margo—you are now the hostess for the annual World Oculists' Convention near Mexico City. We've published your photograph in all the newspapers.

GENERAL: Congratulations.

MARGO: Thank you.

JEWELLER: As usual, the oculists' affair is held at the legendary Hacienda Ramon. Your friend is in the neighborhood. He'll see your photo. He will come. He won't leave the stone behind, and I'll hear it singing in his pocket. It belongs in my forehead, a dim glow in the darkness of the temple, the incense spirals upward… Pardon my enthusiasm. Hmmm. It seems my new associate is late—or perhaps…

TRANSLATOR: Café con leche, por favor.

WAITRESS: Got it. Anything else?

TRANSLATOR: Yes. Some jello, please.

WAITRESS: Red? Or green?

JEWELLER: *(To* TRANSLATOR*)* Are you the taxidermist?

TRANSLATOR: I'm the translator.

JEWELLER: Who?

TRANSLATOR: I mean, no. I just stopped in for a drink on my way to…

JEWELLER: Thank you—Margo, you look lovely in this light. You remind me of someone

MARGO: Really? How interesting.

JEWELLER: Do you play the flute?

MARGO: No.

JEWELLER: You could learn.

MARGO: Can I get another coco-loco?

JEWELLER: Of course… You know, I'd planned to immure you forever, along with your clever boyfriend, in the Green Vaults of Dresden. I even brought my trowel along. But I've had a better idea.

GENERAL: O God. I would hesitate to present you raw recruits with my informed speculation as to the nature of this jeweller's revenge. However, familiar as I am with illegal conduct in the line of duty, I have begun to prepare my alibi.

TRANSLATOR: "'When the fog is heavy on the road to the Emperor's Jewelled Garden, you hear voices all around you, shouting directions. Go South. When the fog burns away, no sign of travellers—no horses, no carriages, no tracks in the dust.' The man in bandages stopped talking, stood up slowly and walked over to the window…"

WAITRESS: Anything else?

TRANSLATOR: Uh…say, Miss…I'm a stranger here, and I thought you might … have a drink with me after work.

WAITRESS: I'd love to, cowboy, but we never close.

TRANSLATOR: What? But you can't mean that you…

WAITRESS: Will that be all?

GENERAL: *(To Margo)* You're thinking about him, aren't you?

MARGO: I think about him all the time.

GENERAL: I was married once. I loved my wife. Loved the children.
One day, after we'd been married for ten years, when I came home from work my wife kissed me with surprising passion. She'd bought me a present—some kind of aftershave. That night, in bed, she was heaven. She did everything I liked best, and that woman knew me. I fell asleep full of renewed hope for our future. The next morning before I left for work, she wrapped her arms around me, as if she never wanted me to go. Finally I got to the garage, got in my car, turned the key in the ignition, and the world exploded. She'd had her boyfriend wire a bomb behind the dashboard. I

almost died. I had so much glass in my face it took the doctors two weeks to get it out of me.

MARGO: Why are you telling me this?

GENERAL: So you'll understand.

MARGO: Understand what?

WAITRESS: What'll it be, folks?

*(*ED *comes out of the kitchen, goes to the* TRANSLATOR*'s table.)*

ED: Hello, slick. Got a cigarette?

TRANSLATOR: Sorry. I don't smoke.

ED: You new in town?

TRANSLATOR: Well, I…

WAITRESS: A Blue Plate Special, heavy on the gravy, Enchilada combination, and a coco-loco.

ED: I quit.

WAITRESS: Don't tell me. Tell your mother. Tell those nice folks at table ten.

ED: The hell with them. I gotta get my ticket. *(Ticket windows)*

TICKET SELLER: How many?

ED: I'm a first class grill man, a soldier of fortune, and a doctor of medicine. You happen to be looking at the inventor and sole distributor of Deep Sea Ed's analgesic balm, an unfailing cure for mumps, measles, malaria and all other diseases beginning with the letter M.

I am also an artiste—sole inspiration and executor of Deep Sea Ed's Hall of History, a faithful and three dimensional panorama, a solemn reminder of the grandeur of bygone days, including a diorama of the glacial age of the cave man, constructed under the supervision of college professors; a tableau of the

hideous murder of Prince Kanitovsky by a bellboy at the Connaught Hotel; a complete model of Ford's theatre, featuring the great President Lincoln, and his vile assassin, John Wilkes Booth!
I made all these figures that you see before you, in poses taken from the life. Lessons to be learned! Not only entertaining, but educational as well!
Hell, that show is what you call defunct.
It's a moving world, my masters, and the sands are forever shifting.
The Central Labor Service down on Avenida Juarez got me connected near Mexico City. World tells you something, you go along.

TICKET SELLER: I'm not interested in philosophy. I'm interested in selling tickets. What's the situation?

ED: Through the sharp hawthorn blows the cold wind.

TICKET SELLER: Too bad. What are you doing about it?

ED: Going south.

TICKET SELLER: How many?

ED: One, please.

(MARGO *to the* TRANSLATOR'*s table.)*

MARGO: Hi.

TRANSLATOR: Hi.

MARGO: You know, there's only really two ideas about the things people believe. One is—only the stuff everyone believes is true, like the sun is wonderful, and there's probably some kind of God inside, and hurting people isn't nice…that stuff. The alternate choice is: If every one believes it, how could it be true? I mean, it's obvious that everyone else is not too bright, and that only the stuff I believe is true. I mean, if anyone agrees with me about something, I start thinking my idea must be pretty stupid. Do you agree?

TRANSLATOR: I…

MARGO: Shhh. I'm being kidnapped.

TRANSLATOR: That's, uh…too bad.

MARGO: They want my boyfriend to come for me.

TRANSLATOR: Where are they taking you?

MARGO: They didn't say. Oh, yeah—a hotel in Mexico. The Hacienda Ramon.

TRANSLATOR: What a coincidence. That's exactly where I…

JEWELLER: Ah. Here's the taxidermist now.

TAXIDERMIST: Listen carefully, so that when you bring me the skin you won't have marred all. In preparing lifesize mounts of men, a cut should be made from the throat to the crotch in the underbelly. Then cut in from the center of each palm to this main cut. Peel this thief's skin back, and off completely. Skin the feet out to the last joint in his toes. Proceed in the face area as for antlered animals.

MARGO: He isn't antlered.

TAXIDERMIST: Wash any blood off with cold water. Salt the skin thoroughly. Let drain, salt again. Regular table salt will do. Diamond Crystal, for example, is fine.

JEWELLER: General, write that down. Diamond Crystal.

TAXIDERMIST: Do all this, and bleach out the bones. I will articulate and mount him with pleasure. Half now, half on delivery.

JEWELLER: Nothing now. I need to see the work. It's going to be complex. He won't be complete.

MARGO: You'll need to improvise.

TAXIDERMIST: Who's plaything is that? What is she saying?

JEWELLER: She has been refusing to accept her ... situation. Her mind is playing tricks on her.

GENERAL: She's the bait.

MARGO: I'm a nurse—in this clinic. There. How easily we communicate when we're in the same context. We understood each other, just for a moment. Isn't that fun. *(To herself)* I'm beginning to think these patients are making sense. A bad sign.

DOCTOR: Nurse, relax. You've had a long day. Have a cigarette while I check the ward. The box is full.

MARGO: The darn thing's a paperweight.

JEWELLER: That's exactly what it is.

MARGO: Oh God. I miss my playmate. Did I tell you about him? The Unseen Playmate. You have one of those? You know what I remember about love? When She is disfigured, He blinds himself. And vice-versa. When He is disfigured, She blinds herself. Uh oh. I better read my book. It calms me down. It's a silly adventure story.

JEWELLER: In the Book of Brightness, Rabbi Isaac the Blind mentions the two causations: horizontal or "one thing after another" ...and vertical. There are no accidents, says Rabbi Isaac the Blind.

MARGO: I'm off duty now.

TAXIDERMIST: She's delightful. When you're done with her, perhaps I could...

MARGO: You. Go home. Sort the bones.

JEWELLER: The man in the next bed to mine has these dreams where he is in a dark place, red and green lights in the distance

GENERAL: Ah! Service!

(Waitress is heading toward them. Music. They're gone, and she is the barmaid.)

18.

THIEF: I'm in this bar in Hermosillo. I couldn't stay with Deep Sea Edna forever, but I took her advice.

EDNA: Buy a butterfly net, and go to Mexico.

THIEF: Yeah. No one would think that a crazy gringo is wandering around with a ball of fire around his neck... You know I go through these little Mex towns and sometimes I think that these people sitting around the Zocalo can see my thoughts 'cause the stone is shining in my head and they can look right in and see it...and one of them is gonna say...

MAN: Beer, Señor? I myself am very interested in red and green butterflies.

THIEF: ...and lead me down this alley and a coupla guys with pigstickers are gonna emerge from a pink door while Marty Robbins sings *El Paso* and I'm gonna be in a big puddle of blood, and I'm not only gonna be there, I'm gonna stay there. So I'm a careful traveller...down through Enseñada, Guaymas. Here in Hermosillo, I got nervous. I hired ten guys to dress up like me, gave 'em butterfly nets, told 'em to go to the public library and carry books around town, so my image would drift confusingly around these dusty streets, past the statues of generals... Or did I dream that? ...I'm in this bar in Hermosillo, the Platillo Volador. Sitting at the bar next to me is a guy from America, and it seems to me I've seen him somewhere before. He looks like a pool hustler from Indianapolis and I'm not far wrong as he's from Grand Forks, North Dakota. I open the conversation. How you doin'?

ED: Behaving.

THIEF: And I gotta think about that one. I figure he wants me to know that right now he is not in a Mexican whorehouse, or chasing the waitress around the tables while his wife sits in North Dakota screaming at the kids. But he wants to imply that he could be going wild if he wasn't exercising control. He's got the potential.

ED: Hey—Teresa. Gimme another, will you.

TERESA: You got it.

THIEF: Then I understand what he meant. He just wants to tell me he's "behaving" like exhibiting behavior, like at the zoo—and implying that I should watch this with some attention and I might learn something. Just see him lift his glass, slide his elbow forward on the bar, sit back and breathe. Just breathe.

ED: They could put me in jail for what I'm thinking about doing to Teresa, but they won't. They can't find out. It's inside my head.

THIEF: Yeah.

ED: What's your line of work, Mister…

THIEF: "Mister Raven" I tell him. I'm a dealer in precious stones. He'd look at me like I was crazy, but he don't, cause he isn't listening. *He* wants to tell *me* something.

ED: I been around the world. Three years in Thailand, two in Japan, all over the U S A. I been in France, England, all those places, and you know what? This town we're in right now, this is the best damn place in the world.

THIEF: I think that one over. Well, I don't know, I mean, I'd like to be somewhere else. I have this girlfriend and I find this place a little scary.

ED: You're wrong. I been around. I know. This is it. Best damn place in the world.

TERESA: Teresa brings him another.

THIEF: He tosses it down, leaves a pile of pesos on the bar, and stalks out, all before I have a chance to agree with him.

TERESA: Teresa hands the Thief a newspaper.

THIEF: Hey...Margo's picture. Its her. I quote. "The Oculists' Annual Trade Fair and Exhibition will be held, as usual, at the exclusive Hacienda Ramon, Miss Margo Lamont will present the Oculist of the Year award at seven in ballroom E. Party at eight. There's more...

(All arrive at Hacienda Ramon: EDNA, GENERAL, JEWELLER *and* MARGO, *and then the* TRANSLATOR.*)*

THIEF: The Hacienda's electric garden is open to the public between three and six P M. At this moment, on the terrace adjacent to the main dining room, two men are deep in conversation. Continued page 101, column 10.

TERESA: Will that be all?

THIEF: No. There's more. I gotta bring something somewhere. I gotta meet someone. *(He is gone.)*

TERESA: Hey—you forgot your butterfly net.

19.

ZENDAVESTA: Have you taken the tour?

TRANSLATOR: Mister Zendavesta, you said there'd be peace and quiet down here, that we'd have time to work on the translation. You've done nothing but dance with the wives of oculists from Detroit till dawn. You're never in your room. Look, I have to be honest with you. This text is either so corrupt with modern emendations that further work on it is pointless, or I am simply incapable of…

ZENDAVESTA: Have you taken the tour?

TRANSLATOR: No.

ZENDAVESTA: Take the tour.

TRANSLATOR: I don't think you understand. This supposedly third century B C text has a fragment in it in which a jeweller and some companions take a train ride. It's like translating some kind of grade B adventure story. This can't be the book of the Yellow Ancestor. Yet, there's something about it that…

ZENDAVESTA: These oculists, all around us…don't they seem to you to be somehow—wonderful?

TRANSLATOR, Look, I've been trans…

ZENDAVESTA: No doubt you're an intelligent young man, and I appreciate your efforts, but I'm no longer concerned with how they—end. Keep the manuscript. Translate it if you wish. Its secrets no longer matter to me.

I'll be frank. For most of my life I assumed that those men and women I saw around me were contraptions, not people with feelings like my own. I planned to escape them by creating a universe of my own, and moving there.

But this convention has opened my eyes. I was sitting in the Tropical Lounge, in this very hotel, the night I arrived, alone. Upstairs, at the desk, the first oculists were checking in. The bartender was missing two of his front teeth. I had a stomach ache. Then suddenly, I understood the truth. That evening, in the Tropical Lounge at the Hacienda Ramon, by divine miracle, nerves of God had been projected into my body. God's semen, you see, in the form of divine white nerves, has extended down from heaven and pierced my form. Impregnation has taken place. There is no longer anything I want to know, or any place I want to go. I have enemies, however. Plans are being made at this very moment to abort the sacred seed, by pumping out my spinal cord. This they intend to do by means of so-called little men, placed in my feet.

TRANSLATOR: You are totally out of your fucking mind.

ZENDAVESTA: Take the tour. I think you'll find it instructive.

TRANSLATOR: What tour? Where are you going?

20.

MRS LAMMLE: Do you mind if I sit down? I couldn't help overhearing your conversation. My name is Mrs. Carl Lammle. I'm not interested in philosophy. I used to be, but now I think it's a lot of shit. I just want to talk to someone.

TRANSLATOR: I'm someone.

MRS LAMMLE: Good. I'm here with my husband—Carl. He's a professor of the retina or something. Very disciplined, Carl. We've been married for twenty-seven years. Carl's a member of the Rotary Club, hasn't missed a weekly meeting for those twenty-seven years. He went to a meeting yesterday in Mexico City, doesn't speak a word of Spanish, and there were all these Mexican Rotarians saying things he didn't understand, and shaking his hand. He came back very pleased. We have a son. His name is Fred, and I don't tell you this to make you feel bad for me. He was born with brain damage.

He's twenty-six years old now. Carl goes to this clinic in the mountains every weekend, to shave him. Fred never recognizes him. I stopped going years ago. You know, people say I look all right, but inside, I'm a basket case. Last night I woke up about two a.m., thought I was sick. I was covered with sweat, racing inside like a car engine when the accelerator's stuck. I even got dressed and went down to the Tropical Lounge. Nobody around but the bartender. Some Mexican song was on the jukebox. It made me cry. Sometimes I think that nothing's happened for the past thirty years, except inside my head, and that's always repeating itself. I used to write articles for magazines, and believed I knew things other people didn't know, and that they should find them out from me. That's a lot of shit—don't you think?

TRANSLATOR: I don't know.... The most amazing thing about this place is that even when I close my eyes, and then open them again, it doesn't go away.

MRS LAMMLE: You think that's amazing?

TRANSLATOR: Well...yes.

MRS LAMMLE: Fine. Ah. Room Service. I want to tell you a story. There's no point, really. It's part of my life and very simple. When I was a young girl, I got a job demonstrating gas stoves for the Magic Chef stove company. This was in the depression, and people didn't have much money to buy food, much less gas stoves, and I was selling them in Oklahoma, which was worse off than most. But it was the time of the oil and gas boom down there. Lots of people whose land was crossed by pipeline were allowed by the companies to tap into the gaspipe for free. So they were a pretty good market for the Magic Chef range.

I had a driver, who also did my grocery shopping and rented the town theatre, where I'd put on this cooking show. I memorized certain recipes and had practiced, so I did 'em just right on the Magic Chef. I'd pass the results around the hall on paper plates. Those people would figure a pretty young thing like me couldn't cook that well, so the stove must have done it. And they'd buy. I'd do all this cooking dressed in a gypsy costume. I'd do a few simple tricks too—color changing scarves mostly. After all, it was Magic Chef. I did that for two years. What do you do?

TRANSLATOR: I'm a sort of writer.

MRS LAMMLE: Are you going to put me in a story?

TRANSLATOR: Don't worry. I'd never put you in a story in a way you wouldn't like.

MRS LAMMLE: What way wouldn't I like? Its all the same to me.

21.

JEWELLER: General, the ballroom is ready. The party begins. When the Thief appears, searching for Margo, approach him cautiously. Some casual conversation...

GENERAL: Good idea.

MARGO: Yeah. Let's talk to him. I've got a few things to tell him myself.

JEWELLER: Soon, I'll meet him. I'm no longer sure what I will do.
A man may wander, unaware, into murky windings underground, from which he may never emerge. The Zohar tells of three men who determined to explore this realm of darkness. They descended. One still clings in terror to the wall near the entrance, too fearful to move—one went mad, and disappeared among the pathways of the black maze. Only the third, Rabbi

Isaac the Blind, returned safely. He claims to have met himself, and led himself back to the upper world. *(Music)*

(The Ballroom. Music. All characters except the THIEF *appear. Cook emerges from his kitchen.)*

ED: Edna!

EDNA: Ed!

(A stately dance, during which the THIEF *arrives, and places the diamond on a pedestal among the dancers. The dancers stop their movement.)*

MRS LAMMLE: Just how I like it.

EDNA: Right in the sight lines.

MARGO: Very up-tempo.

MRS LAMMLE: Under control.

GENERAL: And on the level.

JEWELLER: Just how I like it.

ZENDAVESTA: Perfect. Just going through the motions.

MARGO: Exactly. I want my life to be so pure I'll get death threats from the public.

ED: You got anything worth safe-keeping, leave it with the Fat Boy. He never leaves his chair.

THIEF: I like to spend my money on things that disappear—liquor, food, drugs.

TRANSLATOR: Things that come and go.

GENERAL: Sex is barely worth dropping my pants for.

ZENDAVESTA: Just going through the motions.

MRS LAMMLE: Up tempo.

ED: Under control.

WAITRESS: And on the level.

THIEF: Just how I like it.

ZENDAVESTA: Have you taken the tour?

MRS LAMMLE: The flying figure of a mutilated man? Yes, last night…

JEWELLER: What a coincidence.

MARGO: Leave it with the Fat Boy.

WAITRESS: Is the guest of honor here yet?

GENERAL: Who is he?

JEWELLER: I don't remember.

THIEF: I just feel good.

MARGO: Why?

THIEF: I don't know why.

EDNA: Good feelings from nowhere, that's a sign of death.

ED: Right…things that come and go.

TRANSLATOR: The flying figure of a mutilated man. Last night…

EDNA: Perfect. Just going through the motions.

MRS LAMMLE: That right. Certain portions of my brain are being held hostage.

WAITRESS: Red or green?

TRANSLATOR: At this moment, a limping Persian is passing by the wharf.

MRS LAMMLE: At this moment, a plate of food is being soiled by the shit of two rats.

ZENDAVESTA: At this moment, one hundred and one emaciated monks are holding up their broken fans.

JEWELLER: At this moment, the black turtle climbs up the candlestick.

EDNA: At this moment, the bride is facing her husband, the old man is feeding his grandchild. The bottle is warm in his hand.

GENERAL: What a coincidence.

THIEF: Things that come and go.

MARGO: Just how I like it.

ED: Leave it with the Fat Boy.

GENERAL: I'm not interested in philosophy. Just tell me how it ends.

EDNA: I'm not interested in philosophy. Just tell me how it ends.

WAITRESS: I'm not interested in philosophy. Just tell me how it ends.

ZENDAVESTA. I'm not interested in philosophy. Just tell me how it ends.

MARGO: I'm not interested in philosophy. Just tell me how it ends.

ED: I'm not interested in philosophy. Just tell me how it ends.

MRS LAMMLE: I'm not interested in philosophy. Just tell me how it ends.

JEWELLER: I'm not interested in philosophy. Just tell me how it ends.

THIEF: I'm not interested in philosophy. Just tell me how it ends.

TRANSLATOR: I'm not interested in philosophy. Just tell me how it ends.

(Ride out.)

(Sound out.)

(End ride.)

VOICE: Those who wish to ride again, stay in your seats. A man'll be around to take your tickets. Those getting off, step lively. Exit to your left or to your right.

END OF PLAY

NOTE ON STAGING

The text of DARK RIDE includes a minimum of stage direction, and a minimum of description as to set, costuming, and design. This is for two reasons. All the necessary information as to place and the movement of actors can be inferred from the character's dialogue and the stage directions given—and because of the author's wish that the play be adaptable and responsive to particular actors, directors, and playing spaces. The text should be thought of as a basic ground, out of which the staging should grow. There is no "right" way to stage DARK RIDE.

I would like, despite my desire for anyone working on a production of DARK RIDE to allow their theatrical imaginations full rein, to make some thematic and practical suggestions.

The idea of a "dark ride," or carnival spook or ghost ride through a funhouse, where images and scenes appear suddenly out of darkness and just as suddenly disappear, is helpful to keep in mind: lights in the dark.

A cinematic approach, where scenes fade into one another, or are cut to rapidly, would also be helpful to think about. The lighting should be hard, colorful, and jarring, like that of a seedy carnival: lights to look at, as well as lights to light the scene.

Settings can be simple. Rather than using large set pieces, place can be indicated by props that easily move on and offstage. The use of projections, video and sound to establish place and mood is also possible.

The text offers within itself many visual suggestions. Often all that is necessary to establish place is the language alone. If the director thinks more of the techniques drawn upon to stage a Shakespeare play, soliloquies to the audience and all—rather than a nineteenth or twentieth century drama, he or she will be closer to the mark.

It is also of interest, in a piece like DARK RIDE, to stage certain moments of thought or memory as well as, or as an overlay to, the present time-place of the action.

Also, the director and performers should be aware that DARK RIDE is a weave of tales, of scenes within scenes, like the facets of the diamond. That a scene is within a book, or a picture, or in someone's mind makes it no less "real" in terms of staging. The "real" point of view is a shifting one.

The following scene list may be helpful as well.

ACT ONE

1. The Dark Ride begins/introduction

2. The Translator at home

3. Margo at home/at the clinic in her mind/with the Jeweller, Head Nurse.

4. The Thief at the Embers Cafe/with Waitress and Deep Sea Ed as cook.

5. The General on T V

6. The Translator again

7. Thief at the Embers/Deep Sea Ed and ticket windows/Waitress

8. The Jeweller in his office/with Thief.

9. The Thief at Deep Sea Edna's motel.

10. Mrs. Lammle at a lecture hall/all as audience and demonstrators

11. The Translator and the Thief at Mr Zendavesta's oculist shop/occult bookstore/with Mrs. Lammle.

12. The Jeweller and the General at the Jeweller's office

13. Margo at home, with Jeweller and General

ACT TWO

14. Mrs. Lammle's lecture hall

15. The General, Jeweller and Margo on the way to Mexico/train with Conductor

16. Deep Sea Edna's Shooting Gallery and Marine Museum, with Thief and Mr Zendavesta

17. A cafe near Mexico City/Deep Sea Ed's ticket windows/ echoes of the clinic—Waitress, Translator, Ed, Jeweller, General, Margo, Taxidermist, Head Nurse.

18. A bar in Mexico—Thief and Deep Sea Ed

19. The Hacienda Ramon

20. The Hacienda Ramon

21. The Hacienda Ramon

22. The Hacienda Ramon—ballroom

23. The Hacienda Ramon—ballroom/end of ride.

PROPERTY LIST

This is the prop list from the original New York production, and indicates its special concerns and style. The hope is that this list will prove suggestive, and open to strong changes, additions, deletions. This production also utilized two moving projection screens, one 10′ x 13′, and another 6′ x 14′, and the projections used were not only of "place", but of visual ideas, memories, etc.

Scene 1:
"You Are Here" light box sign
Five carnival lights on stands
Two large projection screens
Ride ON/OFF switchboard with lever
Crate

Scene 2:
Manuscript *Book of the Yellow Ancestor*

Scene 3:
Book
Hospital chair with restraints
Postcards

Scene 4:
Vertical highway stripe-light box
Ice cream sign-light box
Small leather bag with flashlight in ("diamond" within)
Cafe table with plexi top-light box
Ketchup, salt, fork etc.

Pie display case with jello, pies, eyeglasses
Menu
Cooks cage with warming lights
Clock-light up face
Cooking utensils
Order pad
Cigarettes
Two folding chairs

Scene 5:
Pointer
Book of Intelligence

Scene 7:
Mummy of John Wilkes Booth
Bus ticket windows
Tickets
Money, for Ed

Scene 8:
Large faceted diamond in leather bag
Chair

Scene 9:
Motel sign
Two folding lawn chairs
U F O Review
Key with room tag

Scene 10:
Cardboard fish
Cardboard handkerchief
Goose
Window frame with curtain and shade
Small fish
Two 3″ green taxis
Two 3″ male figures
Podium
Small American flag
Coincidence scrapbook

Scene 11:
Diamond Oculist/Sublime Publications sign
Eyechart on castered platform-light box
Two rocking bookcases
Hospital chair
Eye-exam instrument
Eye glasses display
Bell

Scene 12:
Zohar book
Pointer

Scene 14:
Bible
Charlotte russes
Spoons, tray

Scene 15:
Dispatch
Postcards
Three chairs (on train)
Train tickets
Camera
Cow skull

Scene 16:
Rocking clown face
Line of cut out shooting gallery ducks
Two lawn chairs
"We Live Inside" pamphlet

Scene 17:
Two tables
Four chairs
Two coco-locos, tray
Book (Margo's)
Silver cigarette case
Two taxidermy animal cages
Bus ticket

Scene 18:
Bar sign-light box
Two chairs
Newspaper
Butterfly net
Two lines laundry
Drinks, tray

Scene 19:
"Welcome Oculists" sign on stand

Scene 20:
Charlotte russe tray

Scene 22:
Pedestal with light within
Large jewel